VAUDEVILLE IN THE DARK

For Deb & Henry

Vaudeville in the Dark

POEMS

R. M. RYAN

Such dear, dear friends. I love you.

Rick
10: 2010

LOUISIANA STATE UNIVERSITY PRESS

BATON ROUGE

Published with the assistance of the Sea Cliff Fund

Published by Louisiana State University Press
Copyright © 2010 by R. M. Ryan
All rights reserved
Manufactured in the United States of America
LSU Press Paperback Original
FIRST PRINTING

Designer: Mandy McDonald Scallan
Typeface: Whitman
Printer and binder: McNaughton & Gunn, Inc.

Library of Congress Cataloging-in-Publication Data

Ryan, R. M.
  Vaudeville in the dark : poems / R.M. Ryan.
    p. cm.
  "LSU Press Paperback Original."
  ISBN 978-0-8071-3689-8 (paper : alk. paper)
  I. Title.
  PS3568.Y393V38 2010
  811'.54—dc22

                                                      2010009322

Individual poems have appeared in the following magazines and anthologies:

5 AM: "The Miner's Tale"; Another Chicago Magazine: "Taking Turns"; Anthology of Magazine Verse & Yearbook of American Poetry: "The Accordionist"; Dreams & Secrets: "Hide and Seek"; Exquisite Corpse: "Depression"; Faultline: "Notes on the Marvelous"; Irish American Post: "Poems to Polka To"; New Republic: "The Accordionist"; Pif Magazine: "O Careless Love," "I Don't Know. I Never Did," and "1958"; The Quarterly: "We're Failing Better Every Time"; Smartish Pace: "So That Was the End of the Century," "From the Dead of Winter," "Field Guide to the Night," "Floating Hearts," "Down to Earth," "Objets du Monde," and "So Much the Brighter"; The Southern Review: "Lady With a Jaguar"; Tampa Review: "Cancerous" and "Monet at Sea"; Willow Springs: "Glenn Gould Plays the Variations"; Wisconsin Academy Review: "On the Water."

for Carol

the soul's sweet solace

CONTENTS

Taking Turns 1

PART I

Field Guide to the Night 5
O Careless Love 8
I Don't Know. I Never Did. 11
Hide and Seek 13
1958 15
Cancerous 17
Depression 18
From the Dead of Winter 19
The Miner's Tale 20

PART II

Vaudeville in the Dark 25
Art Lesson 26
Where Is My Wandering Boy Tonight? 28
Moods for Moderns 31
So That Was the End of the Century 33
We're Failing Better Every Time 35
Notes on the Marvelous 36
Late Fall 37

PART III

Floating Hearts 41
The Last Shape Possible 45
Down to Earth 47

The Calling 49

Poems To Polka To 52

Afterthoughts 55

Objets du Monde 57

The Accordionist 59

So Much the Brighter 60

On the Water 61

Monet at Sea 62

Lady with a Jaguar 64

PART IV

Glenn Gould Plays the Variations 67

Taking It In 68

VAUDEVILLE IN THE DARK

TAKING TURNS

Prague

On the square
is a monk
followed by a man
with a briefcase
labeled *Good Luck*   .
and the sun
is behind a cloud
as the tourists
take turns
photographing one another
and the astronomical clock
chimes one, two, three
and the blue doors open
on the apostles passing
click, turn, click
while the skeleton
pulls the bell chord
and the golden cock crows
and the statue of the musician
is forever
in the middle of his strum
and the sun is back
and the beer is golden
and the world
with its days
amid the planets and the moments
goes round and round,
the world
we try to hold
with the Nikon
click, turn, click
goes round
at thousands of miles per hour
and the Council was so pleased
to have the astronomical clock
they blinded the clockmaker

to make sure this would be
the only master clock
or so one version
of the story goes
that we learn on the way
to the store that sells
washing machines
and wine and T-shirts
of Franz Kafka
while the ravens
shriek
at the Jewish cemetery
above the tombstones
where messages are left
beneath pebbles as if the dead
get up at night
to read what we're thinking of
and why, really, wouldn't that make sense?
when tonight, as I write,
a fly chimes
against
the globe of light
in my room
one, two, three
counting out
some hours of his own.

PART I

FIELD GUIDE TO THE NIGHT

Oh, just a sliver of the moon, yes,
in the corner of my study window
and below it, looking up, lost—startling
to see him there—blue shirted—me,

or the reflected me—*him*, I guess,
looking puzzled, as indeed I was,
trying to find my way through
this labyrinth of thought. What

was I thinking of? And then, oh,
for just a second, a song—was it Schubert?—
on a radio station slipping out of tune—
a *lied—Ruh'n in Frieden alle Seelen—*

may all souls rest in peace.
Of course. Music to bring the exquisite up.
Eurydices everywhere.
Though they always go back under. And souls?

Come on. Who really speaks of souls,
or of peace anymore? Look here. I'm now standing
outside. It's the middle of the night.
I have my glow-in-the-dark map of the heavens

and my *Field Guide to the Night Sky* with its plastic
patented StarGazer, and I haven't found
a thing except Orion's Belt, but wait—
there, exactly *there*—an arrow.

Why, that's The Archer, isn't it? I fumble
with my map and its phosphorescent dots,
then go back inside to read my guidebook.
I can't find the stars I've seen. I go back out,

now unable to see much in the dark,
go back in, get a flashlight, go out and try
to read the map. I get dizzy looking close
and far, like someone who's tried to climb too high.

Inside again, I find my constellation
in the book. Cancer—what a coincidence!
That's my birth sign, and there it is, outlined
exactly, though the photograph of the actual

constellation looks like a connect-the-dots
impression with no numbers on the dots.
Oh the stories the ancients had for all those dots.
Hera, Heracles, Hydra, and

"the cluster of stars, to the unaided eye,
a fuzzy cloud, but really a thin spot in the floor
of heaven, the Gate of Men, where souls descended
to be born." What a thought, souls floating

down from heaven, God the light behind
the hole-filled scrim of night. God the Wizard of Oz
shifting the heavy, clanking gears, the spinning
wheels of it. Now it's mostly numbers

the physicists have given us, the stars
like shrapnel from a long-ago ka-boom.
Isn't that like a story from our time—
grim, warlike, scientific? The German

painter Anselm Kiefer has these huge
canvases with the heavens made of painted
ash. The stars are phosphor white,
each numbered with a mad infinitesimal

accuracy. I wonder if the Gate
of Men is still open. If I were charged
with figuring out the night, I'd start with that Gate
and have the souls come fluttering and twisting down,

perhaps with little sails to catch the wind.
My explanation of the universe
would involve water and good humor.
All the souls would end up eventually

at sea, directionless, with their little guidebooks.
They'd look heavenward, trying to figure
the riddle of the heavens out, singing,
as they went along, *Alle Seelen ruhn in Frieden.*

O CARELESS LOVE

It was 1962. I was seventeen.
Jack Frazier and I decided we'd go
to the Jefferson County Speedway
where, we'd heard, we could get beer

and loose girls. This was the year I carried
a Trojan rubber in my wallet so long
it formed itself into the leather
and Terry Rafferty said

I had the only wallet with its own
life preserver. Oh how I wanted
to rescue myself with that Trojan.
I was drowning in a sea of expectancy.

I followed my erection everywhere.
The world blew kisses to my skin.
The air was electric along my arms.
I walked behind that one-legged

troublemaker, who yelled *Come on*
or *Hurry up* as he pointed this way
and that. I disconnected the speedometer
on my parents' '61 Chevy Bel Air four-door.

It was a six—not much Jack said,
getting in, but it was all we had
going for us except the tufts of hair
on Jack's chest that got us the beer

and maybe the girls, who suddenly
stood beside us just inside the mesh fence
between the bleachers and the dirt track.
I can remember the constant shower of earth

as the cars circled that quarter mile.
I can hear the motors and the gears working
their way through the dust. I can see
a '56 Ford Crown Victoria, a '49 Merc,

a '57 Chrysler so battered they were like
bad memories of themselves
circling until it was impossible to know
who was ahead and who was behind

beneath the floodlights hung on wires
that flickered as the wind tossed them about.
What I can't see is the face of the girl
who held onto my arm and yelled in my ear

over the noises of the race. My head
filled with her sweet perfume as she talked.
Beer by beer, Jack and I and the girls
worked our way into the Bel Air and out

into the night on some farmer's lane
for kissing and rubbing and touching
and my cock's shout of *Me Me Me*.
The girl and I were out of the car

and into the bushes and out of our clothes
and I was saying *Oh Oh Oh* and she was saying
He doesn't know where to put it
and I couldn't get to the Trojan fast enough

and my essence was in the air as if
I'd given myself to the world that night
and then I was home, feeling stale and sticky.
I splashed myself with Old Spice after shave

to cover up the smell and the feel
of my secret life and the next day
I smelled like a sailor home on leave
and drove around town in the Bel Air,

its speedometer needle now jerking
around the dial as if it no longer
could identify the exact speed of travel.
These are my teenage years.

My parents don't seem to notice
that the transmission slips
and that there's a slight smell
of vomit where Stevie Cocheran lost

his cookies, along with two hamburgers
and a six pack, inside the passenger door.
But then . . . now . . . listening to Glenn Gould's
version of Beethoven's *Tempest* piano sonata,

I realize I'm having all my years.
Half asleep over my life, I hear
Gould speed through the notes
as if he's throwing them away—

whole attics full of melodies
out the window as if he's looking for
the deeper stuff in all the souvenirs—
some image, some blend of notes

that carry grace, and if not grace,
peace then—peace beneath the unsteady light
where we give ourselves to the world
as we circle in and out of the dark.

I DON'T KNOW. I NEVER DID.

Goose Island. It's 1956.
I'm standing on the shore of the lagoon around it.
In the west is the Rock River on its way

to the Mississippi, the ocean, the air.
Farther west is Mercy Hospital
where my father would die in 1965.

To the east are the railroad tracks and the hill
where I sledded in the winter,
one year so happy I peed in my pants

rather than stop in the dark, in the moonlight.
By the time I walked the mile farther east to home
I shivered so badly I thought I was frozen

and my father, laughing, put me in a warm bath
beside the toilet he would sit on years later
shitting globs of black. "Internal hemorrhaging,"

the doctor said, and taught me how
to inject him with morphine, though my father was so skinny
I sometimes missed the vein and hit bone with the needle.

He tried to scream but it came out a whimper,
my father's voice did, but now he was laughing
as he rubbed me down with a scratchy wash cloth.

"No one ever died of frozen pee," he said.
Goose Island. It's 1956.
I've gone there to fish. I got up early but found

the line in my Shakespeare reel tangled
so I rode my bicycle downtown for new line,
came home, found I couldn't install it,

rode back downtown and arrived, breathless,
later than I'd meant, at Goose Island.
I've laid out the sandwiches my mother made,

arranged my gear and tackle on the shore,
though I now see I've forgotten my hook and my bait.
Out in the water the carp flop occasionally,

breaking the water as if to breathe better.
I don't know why, but I cast my hookless line
into the water and watch the end sink beneath

the algae, barely heavy enough for the deep.
Goose Island. 1956. The carp are still
coming up for air, and I'm at my desk now, in 2007,

my heart beating the way my father's did
sitting on that toilet, his blood turning to shit.
I don't know. I never did.

The Chinese tell the fable of the Mandarin
who, for years, fished with a straight pin
instead of a hook. The Emperor came to see him.

"For what are you fishing?" the Emperor asked.
"For you, my Emperor," the fisherman said.
I raise my pen to the sound of the heartbeats,

barely audible in the empty air.

HIDE AND SEEK

It's Monday
and I'm trying
to find
this poem
when suddenly
I remember—
and I'm nine again
at the Nelsons'
(I can see
the white letters
on the blue sign)
in the sunroom
above the office
playing Royal Rummy
on an oilskin cloth
marked with spades and clubs
and hearts and diamonds
like points
on a compass
until Mr. Nelson
and his men leave
and five or six of us kids
run to the basement
to play (among
the wooden boxes
the coffins
come in)
hide and seek.
Then we hear
the heavy footsteps
overhead
and we're out
the cellar door,
one of us *it*
as the rest

scatter into
the brilliant sunshine
of 1954,
the sun dappling
everything,
so that even the fenceposts
seem blessed
with light
as if
the little world
of Macon, Missouri
might be
a jewel.

Oh, this
is the heavy
poem
I'm now discovering
the week after
my aunt—
who lived in Macon—
died on my birthday.
As she died
she squeezed my hand
in love yes
but also
to remind me later
as I walked out
of the coffined coolness
inside Daley, Murphy, and Wisch
that now I
was *it*
in the sunlight,
the older children
hidden everywhere.

1958

The headless chicken
is running toward the alley
beside my grandfather's house.
Amazing the way it goes
as if it had
serious business,
this chicken
running along in 1958
without a head.

John Avery, who's nine
and four years younger than I,
is coming up the cinder-covered alley
to see what all the shouting's for
and I grab the chicken head
and yell "Look, John, look"
as I run toward him
shaking the bloody head
with its yellow beak, its frozen eyes.
"No oh no oh no"
John cries, putting his hands
to his cheeks, standing frozen there
while the headless chicken runs faster and faster
in circles then slows and leans
into its turn and falls and rises
and falls once more
this time to stay.
John stares and stamps his feet
and seems to be standing on
clouds of cinder dust
as he keeps on yelling "Oh no oh no"
and my grandfather laughs and this
is all a little part of 1958

that I'd forgotten
until today when I got
the smudged color photographs
developed from the lost roll I found
in an old suitcase in the attic,
and here is a shot of my father's
'57 Ford parked in the shed
beside my grandfather's alley,
and here, too, is Pam Hart,
whom I loved more than anything
until she dropped me in 1962,
and Ralph Truesdale, who would die
changing a tire beside the highway
sometime in the 1970's, and my father,
who died in 1965, and the garden beyond
the shed with these roses
blurred in that old slow film,
these roses like smears of blood
from that wind, that wind of 1958.

CANCEROUS

My first wife worked in a laboratory
where they gave cancers to mice
using cells from a woman named Henrietta Lacks
who died fifty years ago, yet left behind
a cancer so pure and murderous the mice
shivered together while they died as if
they died of fear itself.

I was having affairs, and my wife
was falling in love with her boss.

Only once did I visit her laboratory
where she worked amid thousands
of animals all dying of cancer.
I can remember mice, albinos I guess,
with pink, translucent skin
and tumors the size of large marbles.
But what I remember most was this dog
lifting his snout over and over
toward where the moon might be
if he hadn't been locked inside
a windowless room.

             "They cut out
his vocal cords," my wife said,
as she delivered dose after dose
of cancer to a cage of mice,
"to keep him quiet, but he thinks
he still can bark."

             I kept this
to myself for years and haven't spoken
to my wife since we divorced. I don't think
she ever learned about my affairs,
and I heard recently her boss left her
for another woman, and the cells of Henrietta Lacks
must go on somewhere, killing as they live.

DEPRESSION

Boy, we didn't get
the manual for *this*
while we were working on
our Webelos badges.

Oh shit
it really is
just the black
and howling

dogs
that come
when we
call.

FROM THE DEAD OF WINTER

Writing from a place where winter lies
so heavily, the trees alone—their branches
bent as if weary of the air—are visible,
I've tried for hours to tell you what I saw
years ago in a moment when I thought

that the world had meaning and meant it well. I
was on Crete with a friend named Robert. Bored, tired
of ruins whose only message seemed to be
that the past was dead, that all the gods were gone,
we happened on a beach one afternoon

where the sun, reflected in a spray of sea,
broke across some rocks and shaped what seemed
a goddess, who rose to comb her hair, then fell
around, upon, and almost through us like a rain
of light that wedded us to what we saw.

But lost in a labyrinth of second thoughts,
what I saw so clearly and understood
is vague and getting vaguer. Where Robert is—
forgotten, though now I vividly recall,
if not the beach, then the woman dressed in black

who waited by the road that summer night
as if to warn us with her widowhood
that more than just our money would soon be lost
while we strolled by, intent on girls and bars
and whatever in the world it was we wanted.

THE MINER'S TALE

Whan that Aprill, with his shoures soote
in Mr. Hardy's tenth-grade English class—
memorizing the Chaucer I've never forgotten.
Mr. Hardy always said we'd carry it

to our graves—the revenge of English teachers.
The droghte of March hath perced to the roote.
When Mr. Hardy told the story of
the gas station mechanic—back in the dark—welding

—a Vulcan—Flying A the gasoline—
clang, clang—hammering away.
"An English teacher, huh? Listen to this:
And bathed every veyne in swich licour."

He lifted his welder's shield, his face a white mask
outlined by a spray of carbon black.
"I've got poetry inside of me
that I've carried from high school all the way to here."

And commenced to tell the tale of him . . . .
and others, yes, at *the Tabard, faste by the Belle.*
just south of . . . where was it now?
The man in that three a.m. restaurant,

the woman shaking raindrops from her hair.
"There was a time," the sergeant said.
Thanne longen folk to goon on pilgrimages.
The miner out of chances, out of breath

miles beneath Sago, West Virginia,
a Eurydice who's never coming back
no matter now who sings for him.
"Tell all—I see them on the other side,"

Martin Toler Jr. wrote. "JR,"
he signed it, and this the miner's final tale.
"I love you." Dying, he could barely shape the words.
"It wasn't bad, I just went to sleep."

And smale foweles maken melodye.
We'll never get them written, will we ever—
those perfect tales we carry to the grave—
those Aprils, Mr. Hardy, that *perced to the roote.*

PART II

VAUDEVILLE IN THE DARK

Nobody's home on the range anymore,
and discouraging words are heard everywhere.

The straight man is getting all the laughs,
while the trapeze lady complains, "It's hard

working without a net when the lights are out.
I somersault through the air with nothing on

but darkness." Are you as worried as I am?
The roller coaster that went into The Haunted House

amid the laughter and the shrieks came back empty,
and the cards we get from Sulfura Curiousitie,

the Madame of Mechanical Magic Fortune Telling,
say only TRY AGAIN. Well, it's time to go.

The solicitor from the American Council for the Guilty
is here and wants you to increase your pledge, and I?

Why, I was The Invisible Man all along—appearing
and disappearing at will, perfectly disguised

in a pork-pie hat, twill overcoat, and bandages.
And when you unwrapped them—nothing

shaped exactly like a man. *Voila*, baby,
c'est moi saying *c'est moi* before I say goodbye.

ART LESSON

Leonardos of skill
will never catch
what the morning
so perfectly
is clear about.
Even Michelangelo
could not transcend the day
the way the evening does.

Why trouble yourself?
Our tiny wits
are never much
against the world.
"You start out lean
and end with fat"
goes a theory of impasto
and of life, I guess.

But all that paint
is hardly wisdom.
It's more like gravity
and it pulls us toward
the chiaroscuro
of the earth.
We should live a little.
Most art lives less.

Worse, it hardly pays.
Rembrandt was broke at fifty.
What he owned—
sold or carted off,
down to the scallop shell
he used in *The Hundred Guilder Print*.
Bought surely by someone
who must've rubbed it in—

"At least he's got his talent left."
Yes, along with a sharp perspective on
the vanishing point.
But maybe that's
why we stand in thought
before someone's minor version
of the all.
He's not alone

in holding nothing of this world for long;
he just holds his nothings
in a finer way.
No, this *River View*
will never catch the way
the water goes and stays at once
in sunlight's clear confusion.
And this *Pathway Home*

is hardly an improvement on
the one which winds below
that tree-banked hill.
Yet, in our minds at least,
we're walking there
whistling
two descending
notes of Mozart's

that resolve into a third.
We're walking there
and thinking how
someone was kind enough to frame
this roadway
where we walk just now,
this roadway
where we have to go.

WHERE IS MY WANDERING BOY TONIGHT?

Charles Ives
Composer of **The Unanswered Question,** Etc.

He never finished
"The Earth and the Firmament."
Half its sketches
now are missing.

The organ music
he left
at the Central Presbyterian Church
was thrown away.

Meanwhile
Mark Twain died
and Halley's Comet
came and went

and the organ grinder
at the elevated station
played "In the Sweet Bye and Bye"
for the waiting passengers

the day the *Lusitania*
sank. They sang along
sweetly in the twilight
as if singing for themselves.

It was
"Charley with his loving heart"
and distant ragtimes
and parts of hymns

from Camp Meetings
along the River.
His father, the bandmaster,
"would always

encourage the people
to sing their own way.
The fervor would throw
the key higher.

Father had a sliding
cornet so that he
could rise
with them."

It was "Every Sunday morning,
when the chores were almost done,
from that little parlor
sounds the old melodeon."

It was the *Götterdämmerung*
on the 31st of March
and baseball
on April 3rd.

He wrote insurance
and the pamphlet
for the customers
called *The Amount to Carry*

as if he knew
what to take
on the pilgrimage
to the River,

what songs would cheer
the way—
"Old Black Joe"
turning into

"Yes, Jesus loves me."
He married—
who else
was possible?—

Harmony
though he
said
"Every dissonance

doesn't have
to resolve
if it doesn't
feel like it."

When he died
his adopted daughter,
Edith, and Harmony
held his hands

and felt
a "luminous serenity"
as if it were
the River

once again
and bits
of songs
from someplace

else and
someone hailing
from
the other side.

MOODS FOR MODERNS

Now it comes to me:
I walked this street before—
why, it must be ten years ago.
I didn't recognize it
coming up this way
but, yes, I lived
in that very building,
the La Mar, and walked
this way to work and oh—
I remember it now—
I had this vision once:
a man was sitting there—
in that exact window
eating dinner and looking out
benevolently on the evening
coming up around him and me
and all of us, I guess,
and the sunlight came across
the window at an angle, so,
leaving him half in darkness
and half in light, and I thought
this is just how things are,
and I meant to write down
what I thought, but I forgot to.
All I remembered was the phrase
half in darkness, half in light
and I said it to myself over the years
figuring it meant something
though looking now at the empty window
from another angle, it's hard
to remember what I meant then
after so many days and nights
have been over all of us.
                    Why just today,
in a restaurant, I looked up
and saw a boy coming toward me

in a jacket with a label that read
Magic Mountain, and I thought
I was in a dream where the titles
of famous books appeared
on clothing, and I wondered
what The Moods For Moderns Store
will be showing for *Pilgrim's Progress*
or *Beowulf* or *The Turn of the Screw.*
Is this what Keats meant
when he said that the poetry of earth
is never dead? The boy would tell you—
as he told me after turning around
and showing me the back
of his jacket with its portrait
of Sylvester the Cat looking
confident as ever—
that his mom got the jacket
at a theme park.

        It was later
when I saw the La Mar
and stood there a while
as the sun was going down
and wondered where the man was
and what he'd learned
over the years we'd been apart
and then I remembered a letter
Hans Christian Andersen wrote
one evening in Naples about
a contralto who had, he said,
"a heart dissolved in melody"
and I wanted to think
we all dissolved eventually
in what we saw
while the sun was going down
just as it was
coming up
on someone else.

SO THAT WAS THE END OF THE CENTURY

Now that Tony the Tiger
defines great for so many of us,
it's a lot farther away than
full fathom five that our fathers lie.

We moved to a different ocean entirely,
so far from swords and metrics that even words
might turn to pulses along the wire
as we burn up the millennial forests

to light the different parts
of the museum's *Illuminated Man* and see how
his systems work. This might be
life after a fashion if it weren't

for the nameless stuff between the particles,
and the monsters that keep
rising from the deep in some *Beowulf*
we study over and over in our dreams.

Maybe it's more like this aquarium
in the *How the Fish Live* display
than we'd like to admit, and it's certainly
calming to stand in front of the aqua light

with our advanced degrees and our financial statements
watching the levels of the tropical fish
and how they chase and nip each other
and sometimes dart at their images

in the mirrored sides as if they think
they live simultaneously in two dimensions
or that their friends agree exactly
with everything they do. Yes, it's calming

to see how brightly they live
among their shit and their diseases
when it's ten below outside
and the ancient trees we're burning up

aren't illuminations quite so much as warmth.
And it's exhilarating to see how,
for no particular reason, one fish
will rise—soar, even—after a bubble

with what might be joy. Even though
he must know, if fish know anything, that bubbles
burst each and every time they're touched,
he rises anyway, shimmering in the light.

WE'RE FAILING BETTER
EVERY TIME
—from Beckett, somewhere

The candle that
I couldn't hold
to anything

I'm holding now
to everything.
So what

if it doesn't work?
Come—
see how the light

makes its ragged way
into the dark
like an optimistic

overture that knows
even Mozart
turns to silence in the end.

NOTES ON THE MARVELOUS

The light
touches me
everywhere

I think
as the sun
and I

greet one another
from our separate edges
of the great lake

though the cold
does pretty well, too,
fingering me

like merchandise
on sale.
Still, I wave

at the sun
and at the gulls
who rise and fall—

pieces of paper
in the wind,
notes on the marvelous

we can't pin down
except to say
what am I here for

if not for this—
to say the earth
is lovely

as it rolls away.

LATE FALL

This sudden November
clarity. Everything nearer.
Then this dervish
of leaves across the yard,
brown spinning up and down,
how DNA might dance
when the drab
teaches us delight.

PART III

FLOATING HEARTS

I've got this rented Lumina
partway into the woods

and my plant identification book
beside me, along with

my yellow notebook.
I'm going into nature,

starting with just the "white
simple-shaped flowers"

on page thirty-six. There's
Bloodroot and Rue Anemone,

False Rue Anemone and Swamp Dewberry,
False Violet and Star Flower

and, if I get to water,
there'll be Floating Hearts.

Outside the Lumina
is this air filled

with black flies and humidity
and the smell of loam.

The book mentions none of this—
not a word about how

the soil looks braided here,
in the far north, as if the world

is held together
by this embroidery of roots

and I've read that entire counties
are really one organism—

a mushroom, I think—a fungus
reaching into everything.

One time I brought this box
of dried blood meal home

to feed my garden.
According to the label

this "natural product"
is 12% nitrogen, which is

the "most important element
for proper plant growth and greenness."

I guess we always knew
it was the death

of animals that made the earth so green.
A meal of blood—the language exact

for once, yet when I sniffed the box
with its stale, flat smell

of old blood,
I could also smell

the scent of children's breath
and I recalled the taste

of lovers' long last kisses
in the dark before

the night is done.
Breath and blood

nitrogen and green
Tammy Smith and me

kissing in the grass beside
the car, the afternoon

of the solar eclipse
when these slivers

of sunlight, like crescent moons,
were scattered in the shadows

as if the world were wearing
the robes of sorcerers

and that night
when I was in and out

of her and the heavens
were out of reach

as they usually are
and now I remember this:

my mouth dry with the memory—
dry with that stale, flat taste

and I stand up with it all
and walk around my study

thinking about the Lumina
and Tammy Smith,

this wild embrace
of one thing with another,

me finally at the edge
of the pond—hot,

bloody with fly bites,
I'm seeing the simple flower at last—

the Floating Heart
feasting on

its dense
entanglements.

THE LAST SHAPE POSSIBLE

This beautiful—this
shimmering almost—

this husk, this complete
outside, wings and all,

of a dragon fly
empty, lying on my lawn.

This see-through husk
with tiny designs

as if it were
a stained-glass window

to the inside, to the
soul if we used such words.

This husk so light
as if this were

the last shape possible
before it all became nothing.

Do dragon flies
molt and leave behind

this contraption with wings
perfect

for soaring and hovering
and landing so lightly

they can walk
on water?

Where could the dragon fly
have gone

where even stuff this good
no longer matters?

DOWN TO EARTH

The woods today
are filled with birdsong
as if there's something in the air
to celebrate, though the dog

heard some other call and came back
reeking of shit or rotted flesh
perhaps from the dump beneath the scruffy tree
where all but the bones of the dead cows

disintegrate to dirt. The chicory
has never been so purple, or so poignant
in the chill last light of afternoon.
It's the humidity, we say,

or the year or the century—or maybe
it's the way the cows lie down
never to get up again
except as the chicory

wild around that dump. Our smelly dog
has also brought us this sun-blanched
deer skull. He drops it at our feet,
steps back like an entertainer

expecting our applause.
What look like hand-stitched seams
run across the crown of the skull
as if the bones were meant to seal in

something precious that's gone for good.
Or has it? Maybe this
is what the birdsong
celebrates.

I'm closer to the world
the eyes of the deer could say
from wherever they've gone.
We must escape ourselves

the air might say
from where the tongue once was.
Stay in touch
the light says everyday

while at night
the earth plays
Embraceable You
for the dark

for the one we're dancing with
for the song in your head
where you have the tune
if not the words.

THE CALLING

I've been plumbing
the depths
of despair.

Sure it's dark down here
but the shower's
hooked up.

The toilet
will take longer
so you'll have to go

outside.
I'm sorry.
I'm so sorry

I call
1-900-IM-SORRY
and gladly pay

the $3.95 a second.
What would you do?
This after all

is the here and now.
This is the nitty gritty,
where the rubber

hits the road.
I'm trying
to stay upbeat

but it keeps
beating me down
even when I look myself

in the mirror.
"Ace," I say.
"Ace, you're a wonder.

You're a marvel.
You're another star
in the Milky Way.

You've got to let
the giant trapped
inside of you

loose." So I rub
my head, my belly
and I get?

And I get this
question,
this question

I entertain
in restaurants and bars
with me

not having an expense account
so I draw these blanks.
They're damn good

blanks. I have them
framed. I leave them
to their own devices

and I say
does this mean
anything to you?

and I get
this
blank look

back
and I wonder
is this

my calling
this
this echo

calling
and calling
and calling.

POEMS TO POLKA TO

You've convinced me.
I'm buying Universal Life.
That's all there is to it.

No more of this
lurking around the potted palms,
a dead carnation

for a boutonniere,
holding onto
a slender volume of verse,

while these pale women
with pimples
look at their shoes

with broken straps
and try to decide while I
sing my variations

on all the standards.
You be the ragged claws
this time. I'm tired

of going sideways—
grabbing for lunch
and coming up with sand.

Sure, I'm in Artists
Anonymous but I need more
than these twelve steps.

Even when they're giant ones,
I'm never sure whether it's
Mother, may I? or the crack

that broke her back
after she talked me into
the Word-A-Month Club,

saying this will soon be
Shakespeare.
I didn't need that.

I'd already signed up
for the Great Souls
Correspondence Course.

So what if I flunked
the final? They told me
to align myself

not just with
Jupiter and Mars
but with moonlight

and the misty air.
I'll end up part
of the Grand Tableaux:

the Historic, the Tragic,
and Little Me. I'll end as Art—
head covered with pigeons,

hands covered with pigeon shit.
You want to shake on it?
Truth is, the truth is like

verdigris. Kiss that
and it's sour to the taste,
poisonous maybe.

What we really need
are poems to polka to.
Sonnets like square dances

with their allemandes everywhere,
tossing their partners
this way and that

looking up
the skirts
of literature.

AFTERTHOUGHTS

"Where was I?" That's the question,
or is it? Chasing these damned
mercury drops and when we get them
they're gone again. "I'm in Fiction"

someone in another aisle declares.
Aren't we all?—here at the Bon-Aire
working for less than the minimum wage,
playing for drunks, yes, but playing

for keeps, too, under a moon
slender as a glass sliver. It's like a cut
in the heavens. That's it, boys,
the light we might get to

if we behave ourselves,
the light . . . well, it's gone,
along with the snows of yesteryear,
though we've got a tail on those babies.

They're at sea, the way we all are,
the shifting floor beneath us
as if a waiter balanced us on a tray.
Whoa, partner, put your head

in a vise, then let it loose
and the Woolworth's cafeteria
shines like Paris. The Christmas decorations
in March at the Korean laundromat

mean the annunciation is arriving soon
with dirty underwear, or is it
the annulment? Hard to figure. The Wheel
of Fortune only slowly turns

the messages up. OK, I'll buy
a vowel. I mean, it's my money
and no one else can play "The Comb Sonata"
like me. No one, I say, but I'm shouting again

and who's listening anymore
except the shrieking baby someone's
tossed here all covered with dirty bubble bath?
And if not a vowel, a word then. I'll take

a word, yes, though this just now occurs to me:
maybe the last word has already been spoken,
and we're just afterthoughts, bumping around
like those little silver pinballs

that can only stay in play so long
before gravity takes over. Faster, man,
faster. Maybe we can save them yet,
though it's so fast we're passing

everything. Full speed ahead, no
turning back. You're Captain Kirk
and I'm Spock and this
is the *Enterprise*. At warp speed,

we're beyond the place where words
matter, a long time after thoughts.
Uncertain of where we're going, you and I—
why, that's exactly where we're headed.

OBJETS DU MONDE

My fiftieth birthday, in the rain, in Paris
just after we saw Rodin's *Thinker*
stained, it seemed to me, from too much thought.

The owner of the bookstore
we ducked inside to avoid the rain
was frail and out of breath.

Literature's a dusty trade—and smells, I thought
as we headed off to Item Eleven on our guidebook
tour—St. Sulpice. The sun came out

and worked its way across the church transept
just as the 18th-century mathematicians
said it would, though I'm tired

of the official sunlight, weary
of the arched windows, of the mosques,
of the places that charge us for the light—

the high dusty version the priests
order us to see as they guide us upwards
to their idea of heaven. Older and therefore

closer to the ground, I find the earth richer
than the air. My pleasures are more . . . well
. . . mundane. Fewer three-star events these days.

What happens hardly has a rank.
Take the winding street we came upon
(unmentioned in our *Michelin*) with its smells

of roasting chicken, rabbit, and pork;
with its cool fragrances of raw salmon on ice,
of snails, of green beans piled

beside nectarines. The heavier cool
of cheeses, of Brie and Morbier,
Saint Paulin and Reblochon,

of Abondance at sixty-nine francs the kilo.
The chill smell of Chardonnay and beer
in the bistros; and at the end of the street,

as if to wrap all our purchases up,
a store titled simply *Objets du Monde*
and then we were out of it, parading up

some three-star boulevard again
with a golden warrior astride a bronze globe
above us and at our feet, at the Metro entrance,

a poster advertising that *Les Maîtres du Monde*
is playing. They always are, aren't they,
somewhere, the officials collecting

our forms and our money and our bodies?
It was Edith Piaf who pulled us back from this,
back into the market, Edith Piaf singing about

the life of the streets, the life that lasts
not much longer than the arabesques
of chatter among the women carrying baguettes

and babies. A retarded blind man shuffled along,
with a cassette player hanging from his neck
blasting her dusky voice from the rattling tiny

speaker, Edith Piaf threaded through our talk,
our appetites for more. *Des Histoires* of you,
Des Histoires of me, among the objects of the world.

THE ACCORDIONIST

The accordionist
just shows up on the sidewalk
across from where you sit

at your bistro, a glass of wine,
a beautiful girl, a lovely man,
the night in Paris indigo and starry.

The accordionist—the accordionist
shows up and plays these melodies,
these tunes you almost recognize,

these tunes you suspect are for a wedding
on a hot July afternoon in the provinces,
the lavender in bloom, the bride smiling,

the groom sweating, the tables heavy
with pâté and cassoulet and Beaujolais on ice.
You're spinning round as you dance to this music

and lovely yes the lavender as you spin
and this accordionist plays on this indigo night
and sings with his eyes closed of the lavender

this accordionist on this indigo night in Paris
is before you rapping on the table
and holding a tray for your francs.

A tray the accordionist holds for the lavender
oh and the wedding dance and this night
this indigo night in Paris.

SO MUCH THE BRIGHTER

I rode over here on my bicycle,
a tangle of shadows following me along,
as I pedaled into the late western sun to see

the salmon leap where nothing's leapt before.
Look: this isn't Oregon. It's
Milwaukee—Kletsch Park—beside

the Milwaukee River, winding its way down
from Grafton, carrying High Life empties
swirling along on their way to Lake Michigan.

Fifty of us sitting on the banks of the river,
waiting for these farm-raised fish,
some genetic jazz sending them in search

of rivers—any river—this river,
to leave a memory of themselves, and just now
one slaps against the unnamed dam in Kletsch Park,

rising from that brown water, a tremble of ecstasy,
hitting the dam, unable to make it over,
slipping back down into the reaches

of the water. We yell like sports fans for her rising there,
where she shouldn't be, this splendid foolhardy
failure. I think of John and Howard, their ashtrays

filling up as they sat there discussing poetry.
I think of us as I ride farther and farther west,
traveling beneath the leaves—exquisite

incandescences—slow flames—
so much the brighter as they start to fall.

ON THE WATER

How surprising
this afternoon
to look over
the side of the boat
and see our shadows
crowned in light
as if in spite of our
various darknesses
we were heavenly
bodies
all along—
gray saints
haloed
by the light
of merely looking.

MONET AT SEA

En plein air? You bet. Out there every
morning, no matter what, on that little cove
of gravel beach, the surf thundering in
as if to protect its few feet of watery turf.

Can't you just see him staggering down the path
from the town above, lugging the chestnut easel
with its brass screws, the box of paints
and Number Four brushes and, clamped

beneath each armpit, a stretched canvas, covered
with white paint, ready to go, that white
soon to be the Unutterable
in the daily round of light, the glow behind

the purple bruise of dawn, the bright inside
the hazy light of noon. See him setting the easel up,
yes, tightening the screws, yes,
a home-rolled cigarette stuck to his lip,

his fat fingers now around the brush,
the greasy dollops of blue and cadmium white.
He's sweating to get the icy Atlantic blue
too variable to have a name—but Monet's got it

there, yes, the iron sky promising rain. Fast now—,
see, he's got the second canvas up.
The brushstrokes quick, getting down the clouds,
the tumultuous clouds—quick, quick, the brushstrokes

of the tumbling clouds of afternoon, towering
there—that's exactly how it was
until—oh until the tides came in
with some steely water of their own.

Monet suddenly at sea, his vest
lifting in the water like a ballerina's dress,
Monet laughing there, floating out,
as if dancing on the waves—puffing his cigarette—

Monet at sea, trying to hold himself up
and then his canvases there, too—oh look—
all that art drifting toward the light
it saw and tried, but couldn't ever hold.

Monet laughing then. See. See.
"You should pray" is what the nuns commanded
to the boy who slept in the classroom at Le Havre
without ever having his homework done.

"Pray, sister?" Monet would ask them. "Pray?
It's laughter we should have instead of prayers—
laughter as we sink beneath the waves,
laughter as our lives head out to sea."

LADY WITH A JAGUAR

Why, *this* is the very day, isn't it?
Haydn. Sunshine. The sea *shush, shushing* in
as if it wants us to be quiet, as if
it might tell us something of what it knows.

Then, later, the woman in the laundromat—
a little faded, I thought, but elegant,
her cheap clothes worn with a purple style.
A fifteen-year-old Jaguar. She moved here

after her mother died, took care of her
for ten years. It used up all the money.
Just the car's left and this twelve-by-twelve cabin
in what used to be Angelo's Resort

outside Monte Rio. The New Year's flood
came within inches of her door. The people here
are broken mostly, but you know what this crumpled
beauty stood up and said?

"This is the kind of day you want to put
in your pocket. Save it for later. Savor it, see?"
The amazing grace of the days out here.
The flesh failing as certain as anything,

the earth on its slow slide into the sea
yet rising up for no good reason at all
out there in middle space over the ocean—
a man borne up by a yellow parasail

sailing into the blue sky and when
he looks back at me, waving, he must see *me*
in the sky as well and *this* I'm yelling in the wind
this is the very day I mean to save.

PART IV

GLENN GOULD PLAYS THE VARIATIONS

Bach sounds like walking here.
Now sprinting,
now walking again
but stiff legged
like a comic in a silent movie.

Now skipping
like a child
out to spend her allowance.
You can hear whistling,
knocking on a door,
two people holding hands as they run
through a meadow   or toward a bus
or away from trouble.

Silence.
Now what?
Oh, a promenade. The stately slow
processional of an important someone up a boulevard.

Then silence once more.
Another movement then.

Why do I think of water
editing the shoreline,
breaking up the rocks,

down to earth about it,
discovering inside that dull

imponderance   what glitters

as it works its way
into everything
so that all is water

and is still again.

TAKING IT IN

The moth
    on a flower petal

taking something in
    then exhaling

 its wings
together
    then apart

like the slow
  clapping

    of extended joy
I saw in a flamenco once

    when the music stopped
and the dancer

    stood there
      arms overhead—

the silent
      slow clapping

  of hands that barely touched

    heartbeats
for this earth
    its bright air

      for the soft breeze
in touch
      with everything.